THE

LAST

FRENCH

FRY

MARGIE MOORE AMBERGE

D1469152

The Last French Fry is a collection of inspirational true stories, of unexpected encounters, with people that most wouldn't even blink at, let alone care to.

From a hardcore NY Bronx man yelling about Tampax on his cell phone in the middle of a grocery store feminine products isle, to a young girl standing in the dark parking lot of a Lowe's on Christmas Eve holding a sign, "Need a Tree", to a homeless woman saving the last french fry for someone else.

This is where real people and real life, meet those of us just minding our own business.

Margie invites you in to experience her everyday life "nudges," that will most certainly nudge you back.

Everyone has a story.

These are those stories.

And they will make you blink/think twice.

DEDICATION

———⁓⁓⁓———

The Man.
The Legend.

The force behind the decisions I've made since I
was a little girl, grasping his pant legs for balance.

Thank you, for not telling me how to live and treat people,
but for living it out before my very own small eyes
just to absorb like a sponge.

Kryptonite had nothing on you.

This one's for you, Dad.

xoxo

ACKNOWLEDGEMENTS

And for the girls....

You all know who you are.

Never would I have made it this far without you.

Stacie...You were there from the starting line,
on big wheels.

Jill...MCC buddies…
and always showing up for 35 years, No Matter What.

Kimmy...from an unexpected lunch,
to dancing on the porch with Elton John...priceless.

Nancy, for so many unspoken reasons...
and bowling for Lamarca.

You all can fill in the blanks.

Endless love and gratitude.

xoxo

❧ So...

She is pregnant. Very pregnant.

She looks to be about 8 months along as I see her sitting in the abandoned parking lot I just turned into because I am lost).

Then…I am running off to bring her back some HEALTHY food.

Not some cheap crap from a drive thru, but something hearty and nutritious (as a Mother, who can just drive by that….and NOT stop?).

When I return, she eats a few bites of the steak and fries, puts it away, and thanks me.

I am a bit stunned. She barely ate enough for 1, let alone 2.

So, I ask her (with heartfelt empathetic concern), "Do you want something else? I've been pregnant too. I can go get you WHATEVER you are craving…no problem… just tell me what you want."

She hesitates for a second, and then she looks straight up at me and says, "No, I need to save some of this food for the others. It's what we do. We all look out for each other."

Wow.

And sometimes we sit in restaurants and don't even want to share the last french fry.

❧ So...

I go to the same carwash every week, and every time the same little girl is there taking in all the cars (she's probably all of 19).

It's a sizable place and can get pretty crazy.... but she runs her TAIL OFF (all alone) through 4 lanes of incoming cars to keep it all moving (and I'm sure she gets minimum wage for this feat).

As I pulled into one of the lanes today, I could see it was going to be quite the long wait....and that she was dancing circles trying to make everyone happy.

She immediately got some flak from some disgruntled people who AC-TUALLY got out of their cars in anger and wanted to know WHY they were still waiting!! (I was appalled)

She was overwhelmed but kept it together and tried to comfort them all.

I immediately jumped out of my car and ran over to her and simply said, "THANK YOU!!!... I see you are working your tail off for all of us and I APPRECIATE you!!...you are doing an amazing job!"....and then I ran in to pay.

Then, she comes running in behind me, up to the register, and starts waving her finger and shouting "HEY LADY....I don't know WHO you are.... but you made me believe today that there are STILL good people in this world!! I NEEDED THAT!"

I pointed at her and shouted back (because she was SHOUTING that at me), "YOU ARE A GOOD PERSON!!! DON'T EVER FORGET THAT!!"

My friends, words don't cost a dime. We can speak life or death FOR FREE. Everyday. Please choose to speak Life.

If the line is too long for you, just don't get in it.

❧ So...

I had heard many things about this one particular old man in the neighborhood when I moved in.

"Don't EVER go over to his place!!!"

"He is blind, mean, and a scary recluse."

Naturally, I was dying to meet him.

My neighbors were horrified. They said, "he has lived here for 30 years and talks to NO ONE!!!! The last guy who went over and knocked on his door got yelled at so badly that we all heard it!"

I asked them, "did he know this guy?"

They said, "oh, no, he didn't"

I said, "Well, if I were blind and didn't know who was knocking on my door, I might be afraid and ask them to leave as well."

Well, lo and behold, the next day I'm helping a neighbor set up a birthday party on her deck, and who comes out of the house next door??? Yep!!! The "crazy, blind, recluse".

She freaked out. She said, "Oh no!!!...he's going to yell because people will be on my deck making noise".

I said, "Well just say hello and tell him it's your birthday and you are sorry, but people will be making noise on the deck and you want to be respectful of him, and to please let you know if it's too much for him."

You would have thought I was an alien talking, so I spoke up for her.

Amazingly, this "crazy, blind, recluse" replied, "Happy Birthday".

What???!!! She was speechless. I could have picked her jaw up off the deck.

So, I went over and said, "Hey! I'm new here and I don't know you yet. I'm Margie, and why don't you come over and join us?" (I'm pretty sure I was going to see my neighbor completely lose it at this point and be sorry she ever met me!)

But again, he floored us and said, "I think I'd like that." What???!!!

The "crazy, blind, recluse"?????

She went into her house horrified, pacing in the kitchen, and I joined him on her deck and started chatting.

When about 15 minutes had gone by, I excused myself to go in to get him something to drink (89 degrees out and horribly humid!).

My neighbor was standing in her kitchen and she grabbed me and shook me hard and said (with great vigor!) "OH MY GOSH MARGIE!!!!!!! HE HAS NOT EVER, EVER, EVER GONE OVER TO TALK TO PEOPLE!!!! AND HE'S ON MY PORCH!!! TALKING TO YOU!!!!"

I chuckled and said, "He's actually a very intelligent man, and I am having a great time talking to him!"

I went back out, and we chatted for about 20 more minutes.

He only has 1 eye that is barely functional, and in the other one, he is legally blind.

He is wearing this tattered old straw hat, no shirt, and yes...I think old and worn boxer shorts.

I didn't talk about the weather.

I just asked him what the happiest time in his life had been.

I asked him what his greatest fear was.

I asked him what one piece of advice he could give me, if it were the last advice he could give, would be (he is 83).

He opened up like a flood gate, and then I completely understood why he was the way he was.

I don't blame him.

And then he got up, after nearly an HOUR of talking, and said, "Thank you for inviting me up on the porch. Now I must go, before the others arrive for the party, because they do not like me."

He died 2 weeks later.

Intense love does not measure

It just gives.

Mother Teresa

❧ So...

I was out running errands and happened to see a woman about my age standing in the middle of a major intersection with a sign in her hand.

I couldn't just ignore that she was standing there in need, and so I pulled into a parking lot and walked over to her in the middle of the median.

Cars are whizzing by, and I feel as though we will be blown off the median.

She was asking for a QUARTER.

A QUARTER.

25 Cents!!!

Now I know right now that some might instantly say in their mind "Go Get a Job"!!!...but I'm going to stand up and say:

Everyone has a story. I have a story, you have a story, SHE has a story.

To think of how often we all just throw quarters around as if they weren't very valuable....and then to think how SHE has been thrown around all her life as if she isn't valuable enough.

All I could think of was that here was this woman, standing alone, out in the beating sun, with very leathery looking skin from all the exposure of being homeless.... with humility.... asking for a quarter.

Did I give her money?

No.

I gave her myself, and I gave her lunch.

Because once again...

We are all in this together, and we all need each other.

I will never look at a Quarter the same way again.

❧So...

He was slouching on a bench outside the local Dollar Tree, when he noticed me approaching.

A sight that really made you want to cringe, and a smell that made you want to hurl.

I hopped off my bike and went to park it next to the bench to lock it up, when he pipes up and happily suggests that HE can watch it for me while I shop, and I won't need to lock it.

Hmmm. Honestly, the first thought that went through my head was, "he's going to run off with my bike"...

but then I realized I should embrace it.

So I happily told him," Great!!, thanks!"

I instantly saw this guy sit straight up and beam from ear to ear.

His whole demeanor changes right before my eyes.

As I go into the store and start shopping, I'm thinking, "Ok, if the guy needs the bike more than I do, then he can

go ahead and take it". I'm throwing things in the basket, when I start talking to God in my head.

"Ok, God, I don't know why you wanted me to let him watch my bike, but if he needs it and takes it, I really hope you're gonna replace it". (sorry, I just tell God how it is).

I get to the check out and end up grabbing a Dollar Tree gift card at the last minute, to give him if he's still there when I walk out.

He's still there...and

I hear him bragging to someone walking by that he's watching my bike for me while I shop.(they look at him like he's nuts)

And, as I start to walk over, he jumps up all excited and says with SO much pride, "Thanks for letting me watch your bike!!!... no one's EVER trusted me in my WHOLE Life!!!!".

And then I realize that it wasn't about ME trusting HIM... it was about ME trusting God.

❧ So...

I arrive at the DMV in California (if you've not driven in California, let me just say there can be up to 6 lanes of traffic in EACH direction on a freeway...so that will give you an idea of how many people need the DMV!) Not a best-case scenario.

I arrived 45 minutes before it even opened, hoping to be at the front of the line.... only to find out that the line was completely wrapped around the building already. So....I decide I must be the life of the party to "lighten the mood" of those who arrived way before me.

When the doors finally opened, it took me ONE HOUR to get to the counter to even just get a number to wait!

(I was #121. Yes. That's right, #121)

But suddenly, when I got just TWO people away from getting my lucky number...an older couple walked in another door with a young man who obviously was mentally challenged (they had not been in any line). I observed the struggle they had just to get him to the side counter to ask for assistance, when suddenly he just threw himself on the floor in the middle of all these people. (One woman in line said loudly, "if that were my kid I'd yank him up and yell at him to get off that #%$^& floor!!!") They told the man at the counter that they needed to get him a California ID (some people in line were actually mad that they had not waited in line with the rest of us and began to protest). Fortunately, the man behind the counter gave them a number for the next available window.

Ah yes, I was relieved.... until... the young man didn't get up off the floor to go get his photo taken. The parents tried to connect with him and encourage him to no avail. Then his number was called, and his Mother walked to the window, just looking back desperately at the situation.

The Father said, "If you get up and get your picture taken we can go to McDonalds for french fries!"

So I got out of line (just 2 people away from them calling my lucky #), because lo and behold....I had a McDonalds gift card in my purse with a picture of the french fries on the front!!!

I thought, "Who cares how long I've been in line...these people clearly need help and I cannot just stand here and watch this poor man try to help his son."

I went over, knelt down and pulled out the McDonalds card and said to the boy (with all the excitement I could) "Hi!!!! I hear you want McDonalds french fries!!! Look at this picture of them!!!

It's for YOU!!!! Let's get up and go to the counter for your photo and then you can go to

McDonalds for french fries!!!!"

He pulled his head up from staring at the floor and carefully took the card from me, smiled, put it in his pocket and looked at his Dad for confirmation. His Father was also kneeling on the floor and looked at me and said, "Thank You".

Within 5 minutes the boy was up and to the window.

They let me back in line....and when I failed my California Driver's License written test by ONE (yes...in fact I did after all of that) .... the woman grading it looked at me and said, "never mind.... you're good...I'm not counting that last one...go get your photo taken".

Now THAT, my friends, .is nothing short of a God story...because NO ONE gets a break at the CA DMV!!

I know that this was long....but I wanted to share it because I hope it will encourage someone to risk "losing their place in line" to make a difference in someone else's life.

We are all in this together.... We all need each other.

Our job is not to judge,
Our job is not to figure out
if someone is deserving
of something —
Our job is to just show up.

~Margie

❧So...

There he was...peeing in a bush in a parking lot, as I was driving by him... and I got the "nudge".

Oh, dear God.

I'm a single woman, alone...and just trying to turn around in this run down, abandoned parking lot (because I missed my turn to my new Dentist office). I decide to just keep driving (not sure my "single woman alone", is a good case scenario here).

I made it out of the parking lot, BUT my heart tugs. Hard.

And then I am drawn to pull into a McDonald's.

I can't drive any further.

So, I'm in the drive thru line, talking to God out loud in my car (yep, certified). "Ok....I have NO idea what this guy needs, but apparently I need to show up...so what on earth do I get for him?!".

I have NO IDEA why...but I order him a "Happy Meal".

(I wanted to add an ice cream cone, but it's scorching hot in the brutal FL summer sun right now, and he might be gone by the time I get back to him) ....and at the last minute I ask for the biggest cup of ice they have, and a cold bottled water.

He's probably 60, but then again, who knows. 70, or 45??

He's missing ALL of his front teeth (and the others appear to be black... and not be far behind missing as well).

His skin has seen better days, and he is bright red from the brutal sun. His clothes are SO FILTHY, and sizes way bigger than his wasting body. He is the poster boy of "homeless".

So, I go back with my Happy Meal.

I pull over (and honestly, I say a quick prayer that I'm not murdered, but I digress).

I hand him an insulated cup of ice, a bottle of ice water...and then the "Happy Meal".

He begins to cry.

"I prayed for ICE!!!!", he says through streaming hot tears.

Choked up, I say, "I hope I helped you in some way, I didn't know what you needed".

Then, he suddenly advances, reaches through my rolled down window, and grabs my arm as I am driving off.

My heart stops.

"I need a new shirt and socks", he says, with desperation.

Now......!!

Before you start thinking that he is "playing me"... let me just kindly remind you, that WE are not standing in the beating sun, without a bed, running water, a place to pee, or anyone who gives a flip. And however he got there...is not my place to judge.

He is THERE. (and I am NOT).

And... when I was asking God in the McDonalds drive thru line, what on earth he needs.... well...I am not about to question it when he point blank tells me.

I ran into Marshalls and bought him a new shirt and socks.

And I didn't just grab "anything".... I looked for good quality, breathable cotton (guessed his size) ...and yes, in a refreshing blue color I thought would look good on him (as if I were shopping for a family member), and socks that had a lot of cushioning.

I hurry back to the parking lot...but he is gone.

Ugh...!

So, I start to drive down the road, when I come across a group of shade trees...and see him eating his Happy Meal.

(I smile so hugely, I think my mouth might split open)

I pull up, roll down the window, and excitedly say...."I got you a new shirt and socks, here!"

He drops his food, runs to my car, and stands silent for a minute...as he holds the shirt and socks I handed him.

Like it was the holy grail.

He then excitedly rips off his shirt, and whips on the new one...with all the childlike wonder of Christmas morning.

He shouts at me, smiling like crazy, "I love you!!!!! I just wanted to be "presentable", to try to get a job".

(and then my eyes become very blurry, and my heart becomes very full).

My "job"... is not to judge.

It's just to show up.

LOVE BREAKS
EVERY BARRIER
IF
WE WILL LET IT.

~Margie

&So...

I was just out for a long walk on the beach, and I came across one of my favorite things: an old couple who is still holding hands and laughing! (I add "and laughing", because there are plenty who still hold hands, but you can feel the immense distance in the dead silence between them)

He was helping her along the shore, as she tried to slowly maneuver a cane in one hand and his hand in the other. (I think she was holding onto them both for dear life!) But they were LAUGHING together about it!

So, I caught up to them to say hello.

He VERY quickly, and proudly whipped out his wallet and showed off their worn and tattered black and white wedding photo.

PRICELESS!

From the looks of it, it has probably been in the front of his wallet since their wedding day 50 years ago. The smile on their faces at that moment when I met them perfectly matched the one in the black and white picture.

They were definitely, a couple that could have easily graced the front of any popular magazine back then...quite stunning to say the least!!

But in this moment, sadly...I don't think anyone would have given them the time of day. They looked very far from their former selves.

Sweetly, he just beamed about her (and she Blushed!) as if they were still 17....yet she was about 60 years past that ...and on her final stretch. Now 77 and looking NOTHING like the wedding day photo.

But the love in their eyes spoke louder than words or any photo ever could.

You can't fake that kind of unconditional love.

And, money certainly can't buy it.

I high fived her (of course) because that's just "me"....and I said, "You go girl"!!!

So...

I left the house for a walk at 8:00 this morning and realized I had just locked myself out.

Ugh!

I stood there for a minute thinking, "Ok God....what's up with that?!!!

Instead of getting all worked up over it, I turned around and just started walking.

As I walked, I reassessed my plans for the day and thought, "Ok...well maybe I'm going to run into somebody who needs my help"...but I don't know.

All I know is, something good better come out of it...

I'm walking for an hour now, when this woman walks up and says, "Hey, did you hear about the woman who was walking here last week and there was a hit and run? "

I'm like, "NO WAY!" How did I not hear about that?

"Yes, they hit her and then ran over her leg when she fell, and she is in a wheelchair now. She's 42 and doesn't have health insurance."

I'm thinking...holy cow, that's just wrong! Then she tells me there's a fundraiser and auction for her at this bar down the street at 1:30 and I tell her I'm sorry I can't go because I have a full day planned (inside, all I'm really thinking is, "I'm not walking into a bar alone!!).

Here was my full day: Ride my beach bike after I get back into my locked house and change. Yes. Pitiful.

Crazy how things happen sometimes, because the minute I got on my bike and started off.... I heard this small voice tell me to turn around and go to that bar with a check.

Right.

If there's one thing I know, it's when you hear that small voice tell you to go...you gotta do it.

No matter what.

So yes, I rode my bike down to the bar.

And I don't know how many good "Christian" people saw me walk in there. All I care about was that God saw me walk in there (because what He thinks is all that matters to me).

Now, I'm feeling a bit awkward not knowing what I'm supposed to do... but there is an auction going on and so I stand off to the side and ask God what in the world he wants me to do in here!

I get this little nudge of "you'll know when it's time".

Big sigh.

Ok. So, I watch some Jerry Garcia stuff get auctioned off and I'm thinking, "Am I supposed to bid on this stuff? ?!" Really?... When this one item comes up and he says, "this has been in the family of this injured woman for over 70 years and passed down from her roots in Holland, but she is willing to let us auction it to help pay her medical bills".

Ok!

That was clearly my sign to bid!

And I won.

I wrote the check, handed her the item back, and said, "this belongs to you", and walked out of the bar.

I didn't need it. I didn't even want it. But I knew SHE did.

And as I am getting on my bike to leave she comes flying out of the bar in her wheelchair yelling to me.

I turn, and she asks my name. I said, "Margie, but that's not important. You might think I'm crazy, but this small voice told me to come over here today with a check, even though I don't know you or anyone here, and I had no idea what for, but I think God wants you to hold on to that family heirloom as a sign from him that He's got you covered."

And I hopped on my bike and rode away.

✌So...

I pull into Starbucks to run in and grab an iced coffee.

Lo and behold the line is out the wazoo! I think, "Hmmmm....should I stand in this long line?...

YEP!" Lol

And when I FINALLY get up to the next person in line and they say, "next customer", this woman behind me lunges out in front of me and gives her order.

So… I'm standing there thinking..."Hmmmm...ok....did that just happen?!"

A couple of people kind of "growled" and gave her the evil eye, murmuring....and the woman behind me was fit to be tied! (I mean.... Starbucks is serious business people...you can't mess with people waiting for a caffeine fix!)

So, I just stand there and don't say a word....no biggie...I'm next again.

Then someone in line YELLS at this lady (and the cashier helping her) that she cut in front of me and

I was supposed to be next! (and the packed Starbucks line is all nodding to back him up)

She was horrified. (I was horrified for her)

I said, "don't worry about it.... it's ok". (Sadly, I got some evil looks for that.)

And when I started to walk away with my order this woman ran up to me with tears in her eyes and said, "I'm SOOOO SORRY!!!!... I was in another world and I normally would have been paying attention.... but my only Son just graduated and joined the Marines and I am a wreck!!!"

You know what? I grabbed her and hugged her.... sobbing in the middle of a crazy busy Starbucks.

I get it.

We all need to "get it".

Someday, we will "need it".

"If we gotta start somewhere,
why not here.
If we gotta start sometime,
I say now."

Toby Mac

❦ So...

We all have a story.

But who has enough time to stop and listen...without judging?

I think, if we could see people from the perspective of their "stories", we could have so much more compassion and ability to embrace each other.

We all need to be embraced.

Right here. Right now. Right where we are at.

For who we are...and where we are at.

No one else's "expected" latitude/longitude coordinates, but right here, right now.

Real love doesn't say "I agree with you".

"Real" Love says, "I'm here for you, right now, no matter what".

No. Matter. What.

I don't believe in "Religion"...I am not "Religious".

I don't believe that showing up in a building every Sunday is going to save us.

I believe that ACTIONS speak louder than words ever will.

Jesus never "demanded" anything.

In fact, in his last dying words on the cross were, "Forgive them, for they know not what they do".

Now... I'm thinking, he should have had every right/reason to yell from the cross something like, "I'll get you all for this!!! I'll make you pay!!!' But he didn't.

I think it might be something to think about.

Seriously.

You treat me like a piece of crap, lead me down a path of haters who spit on me and then literally, drive nail spikes through my hands and feet to force me to die a very slow and painful death on a cross?

He could have screamed obscenities from there. And rightly so!

But He didn't.

He had 7 final statements, one of which was, "Forgive them, for they know not what they do".

I don't know about you, but I think that must have been a REALLY important message.

So...

This woman I met was 70 years old.

SEVENTY.

She was a widow. Married all her adult life to the same man till he died.

She met a kind man last year, a widower himself (whose wife passed from cancer), and they became fast friends.

He proposed a year later.

He brought her to Church with him.

And then they told him that he could not continue to come there if he followed through with marrying her.

When she told me this I was blown away! I said, "OH MY WORD!!!! How devastating for you!!! Why on earth would they do that?!!"

She said, "They told him that I don't wear a bra and speak foul language"

Really?

My friends...

This poor woman is in her 70's and lost her husband of many years, that she was faithful to.

I grabbed her and hugged her SO hard!

I looked in her sad eyes, and asked, "What happened?"

She said, "He went ahead and married me….and then he got kicked out of his Church".

I said, "Oh my word!!! I am SO sorry!!! But what a good man you married!!!"

She was stunned. And then she said, "Well he's right over there in the car waiting for me."

To which I of course responded, "Oh My Word!!! That man needs a hug too!"

She hollered to him to get out of the car and said, "This woman wants to give you a hug!"

So, I ran over as he got out of the car and hugged him so big!

What a cute, sweet, little man!!

Yet so broken, and understandably so.

Like so many of us.

🌹 So...

I think I just had another reality check in the checkout line at Circle K.

It was a long line, and I got in behind this guy who immediately turned around and blurted out to me that he just got a call from his best friend since childhood.

His friend said, "Come pick me up at the hospital. They just told me I have 5 months to live".

They are both 56.

56.

He said he needed to grab a big cup of coffee and think about "things" on the way there.

I think he was in shock. (I was in shock, when he shared this)

His best friend had been the epitome of health, he said, and the quarter-back for their school.

What do you say to that?

But after talking to him and walking back to my place...I really had to think about that. Hard.

Sometimes, we just "assume" that tomorrow will come.

I'm not perfect, but I know there is a perfect ending for all of this.

Unexpected things will happen (even to good people).

You and I, both know this to be true.

I think if we could all just be the voice of Compassion, along someone's journey....

Not judge, but EMBRACE...

What a beautiful thing that would be.

Everyone needs compassion.

And it's Free.

I will show up for whoever needs me until the day I die....and I will share my stories...because, we ALL need someone to "show up".... with compassion that has no "conditions".

I think that's the bottom line.

❧ So...

I have a whole 20 bucks to splurge on groceries today. I am feeling lucky.

Little did I know what I was in for.

It seems as though "homeless" people are coming out of the woodwork today.

It is a Saturday, but it is as though everywhere I turn, there is someone with a sign.

I finally made it to the big Winn Dixie parking lot, but I am honestly overwhelmed after "passing up" so many people. (It can be so easy to forget that they are people just like you and me.)

I am now pushing my cart through the grocery store...

I'm finding it hard to throw anything in the shopping cart.

My head is spinning.

I want to stop and help *every single one* of the people I "passed up".

But I can't.

I grab 2 cans of Campbell's Chicken Noodle Soup (my comfort food of choice) and go out to my car. I sit there, and I think about things for a minute.

And then, I just say, "Ok God...show me WHO it is I'm supposed to help today!"

Lo and behold, as I drive out of the parking lot there is a new guy on the corner…and he has a sign.

"NEED MONEY FOR BEER"

No joke.

THAT is the sign.

And THAT is when I got the "nudge".

So, now…I'm thinking…

What am I supposed to do?? Buy this guy a 6 pack?! (and if so, WHAT brand does he want??)

Boy, does God challenge me with decisions!!

I pass him by, but the "nudge" just keeps pulling me back.

Ugh.

I can't keep driving. Now, I've gotta turn around.

I am literally talking to God, out loud, in my car (yep, certifiably crazy lol)

I pull over into a parking lot…just to, you know, confer with God one last time, before I go doing something stupid…

And, no joke…I look up, and see I am in a McDonald's parking lot…and I get this "nudge" to go in and buy a gift card.

Seriously? The day McDonald's sells beer…is the second coming of Jesus!

Ok.

So now I'm all in.

STILL don't know what I am going to say, when I walk up with a McDonald's gift card and NOT a 6 pack…but hey…I'm gonna roll with it…

(as always...far from perfect, and just 'winging it')

Then, I say, "Hey, I saw your sign as I was driving by...THANK YOU for being HONEST!!!"

I can't really read the expression on his face when I say that...who knows WHAT he's heard people say to him...but here's what just came to me.

HONESTY is ALWAYS the best policy!! (My Dad taught me that)

I used to tell my son growing up, "If you tell me the Truth, I will give you a "get out of jail free card". (I still honor that today)

This guy needed a "get out of jail free card".

I gave it to him.

In the form of a McDonald's gift card...

And as I handed it to him I said, "after drinking all that beer...you're gonna need some food!!"

End of story.

BE SO BUSY LOVING PEOPLE THAT YOU HAVE NO TIME FOR HATE.

~Margie

❧2 So...

I stopped at Walmart today to grab some necessities. Not my favorite place to go...but I took the plunge.

I'm not quite sure why, but I get this "nudge" to give this guy a $20 bill.

So., I walk up and say, "this is a random act of kindness, and today, you're it"...then, I start to walk away.

I am only 5 feet tall ... NOT sure what the heck I am doing...but hey...

Then, all of the sudden, there is a tap on my shoulder.

Now, let me just tell you, this guy looked like the SCARIEST guy on the planet! ... 6'7"...scrappy...sporting facial hair like Saddam Hussein.

I slowly turn around and look up at this towering man behind me.

He looks down at me, hands me the money, and says, "give this to someone who is worthy".

Wow.

My IMMEDIATE response was, "We are ALL worthy!"...

I have to say that in ALL of the random acts of kindness I have performed in my life, THIS was a first.

He said, "Go out in the parking lot...and give it to someone else."

I stood in silence. (silently thinking we both must be crazy)

But I did not argue with him nor disrespect him...and I walked out the door thinking... "Holy cow!!! WHO am I supposed to give this to?!"

Lo and behold, as I am pushing my shopping cart of toilet paper and soap I get a "nudge", to give it to a family I am passing in the parking lot.

Really?

They are driving a Mercedes SUV!!

No joke.

At first, I think, "Oh my gosh!!!...these people will think I have lost my flipping mind when I hand them a $20 bill!!!

So, I keep walking.

But I get this big "nudge", to go back.

Ok.

So...here I am, going back... to look like a COMPLETE IDIOT, in a Walmart parking lot...but I'm going to do it.... because I just "know", somehow...that I have to. And so, I do.

So, I am pushing my cart back towards this family getting into the shiny new Mercedes SUV, when they clearly spot me, heading right for them.

The look on their faces clearly tell me they think I want something from them.

And they, very obviously, start to speed up the process of getting into the vehicle...so I start pushing the cart faster toward them and waving excitedly, as I am calling out.

"Hiiiiii!"

They now look terrified, so I make it quick and, just about out of breath, say, "Hey...this is just a random act of kindness", hand the guy the $20 bill, no big deal, and tell them to have a great day.

He doesn't say a word.

He stares at the money like it's foreign, and he has this blank look on his face.

Then, he looks up and says, "We thought you were homeless and going to ask US for money!"

I laughed and replied, "Thank God I'm NOT homeless!!"

He said, "Well people are always expecting handouts from us, because they see what we drive and think we have it all…but the company I work for just downsized and I am out of a job for the first time in my life."

I said I was sorry to hear that, and I wish it was more than a $20…but something nudged me and told me to give it to you.

Now he looked a little pale, and he said, "you could have handed me a $1 bill…the amount wasn't important".

Just then, his wife stepped out of the car, livid, and asked what was going on!

With the still stunned look on his face, looked over at her and said, "This is my sign", and waved the $20.

She gasped, with disbelief.

He looked at me and said, "I was just SO angry at God and telling my wife, that if there was a God, and if he really cared, he'd send some random stranger out of nowhere to give me money!!!

But she got all mad and said I was being RIDICULOUS…and that would NEVER happen!!

❧ So…

He looked like one of the scariest men I've ever seen, hands down…and he walked up behind me.

I almost didn't know if I could breathe for a moment.

Huge.

Solid.

Probably 6'4".

Full of tattoos… and scars that would make other men wince (and quickly look for an escape).

My brain quickly tried to set aside the sight of him and tried to adjust it, exponentially.

I took a deep breath, then quickly turned to say "Hi".

His face lit up (behind the massive, scruffy beard), and I was instantly, somehow, comforted.

How odd.

And then I noticed the horrific scars on his bald head. It's not like anyone could have missed them, they

are the kind that are blaring in your face and screaming an exorbitant amount of pain… that even Webster couldn't put a finger on.

So, I began chatting with him while we wait. (Me, and all my Pollyanna-like blinders)

What I got, was completely unexpected.

He'd been a sniper in the Army and got blown up overseas. Really blown up.

But here was the kicker.

He said, with what appeared to be watery eyes, (after I thanked him profusely for sacrificing for people he doesn't even know),

"Ma'am, I am proud to have done what I did for our country, I was one of the lucky ones.

I was just a boy from Alabama, with nothing and no one. But today I am blessed, and thankful to be alive.

I tell people who are brave enough to approach me, that I have no

anger, no resentment, for what has happened…. I just want people to understand that it's not about war".

And then he leaned way down and gave me the biggest bear hug I'd ever had.

✌So...

I don't even know where to start, but I know I want to share this story of what happened to me.

I only put myself out there and share my stories so that maybe it will help someone else who has been in the face of extreme difficulty...to have hope....and that God Does Hear Us.

I suffered from some very devastating health issues and secret abuse in my life (beyond my control) that honestly, I wasn't sure at one point that I would survive it all...and I really didn't understand how God could allow all of this when I was a good person and I was seriously doing the very best that I could to serve him.

But in the beginning, when I cried out to God (loudly and literally!) all I ever heard was this small voice coming back to me saying, "Be still and know that I am God". It kept coming back over and over...and so power-fully over the years of abuse that it became my mantra. "Be still and know that I am God."

Friday, I was served divorce papers.

Now, THIS, was NOT how I wanted God to fix things.

I think I walked for 8 miles just hashing through all of this hell over my life with God and praying somehow, he would just show up for me and give me a sign. A HUGE sign, one that I would know... that HE GETS IT... he's always known the truth and I'm going to make it. I wrestled with it all weekend.

First thing Monday. morning, I get in the car with the papers and just start driving around through my blurry tears, to find a Notary somewhere. I pull into a little random place off the beaten path with a sign in the window for a Notary, and I go in. There are about 4 people in there and only the guy who owns the place to run everything. He finally takes my papers and takes me to the back to a super messy counter, opens his notary book, and grabs a random pen out of a coffee cup stuffed to overflowing, with pens to have me sign.

My hand shakes as I take the pen. My eyes are brimming with tears about to spill all over the papers.

I look down, and blink twice.

I am speechless.

I take a step back (as if I've seen a ghost), wipe my eyes, and I ask him with a shaking voice,

"Is this your pen??", holding it up for him to see.

He looks at me odd and says, "it's just a pen...I don't know who it belongs to...they all just end up in this coffee cup. Why??", he asks oddly.

And I say, shaking all over, «I have to tell you my story because this is NOT just a coincidence!!!

I don't know if you believe in God or not, but do you see what is engraved on the side of this pen??! (and I hold it out

for him to see).

"Be still and know that I am God".

He says he doesn't believe in God.

So, I say, "Well let me just tell you my story", and I spill all the beans to this poor guy about all this hell I'd been through and the fact that every time I cried out to God I heard this small voice that said, "Be still and know that I am God".

He stood there, staring at me, speechless.

I told him I had prayed for a sign that God hears me...

"and look at this pen you gave me to sign these divorce papers with!!!" I say with loud excitement!

as I proudly put it out there for him to see.

Engraved in the wooden pen were the words,

"Be still and know that I am God".

Seriously.

How likely is THAT?!

In a random Notary place, in a random coffee cup, on this random day.

And then the owner tells me he doesn't even know where the pen came from, he's never seen it before.

ॐ So...

I go to the same car wash a few times a month.

I'm always amazed at the employees, who truly "kick it up a notch"…no matter what you drive.

I like that.

Not giving better service to someone who "looks like" they have money, but treating EVERYONE, with the same enthusiasm.

And then, a very interesting thing happened.

I had listed my car for sale (Mercedes 350 SLK), and the people who were buying it, were driving 3 hours to pick it up.

So, I told them I'd go have it detailed just before they came.

I went to the same place as always.

But this time, the guy who drove it out of the bay HIT THE CAR NEXT TO IT just as I was walking out to get in it.

Yep.

No joke.

I think I had stopped breathing.

I literally had to stop and try to take the whole scene in.

And then, as any well-grounded woman would do…I lost it.

I broke down crying (no, wait, not crying...but SOBBING) (ok, maybe hysterically crying).

I'm not proud of it, but Yes, I am Human! And it was my "gut reaction".

Today I went back to that car wash because the kid who drove the car out was only 16 and it was his FIRST day on the job when it happened. (He was HORRIFIED, when he realized what he had done) (I saw it in his eyes. The fear of losing his job, when I was "losing it")

At that moment, I was too consumed with sobbing to think straight. Yes, another female trait of mine. I have flaws. All I knew (after I got home and stopped sobbing), was that this poor boy, might lose his job.

It ate at me.

For a week.

And then...I HAD to go see if he was ok.

(yep, it took me that long)

We ALL make mistakes (some SEEM way bigger than others), but in the long run..."it" happens. (and, it's bound to happen! We are not perfect)

But, THAT boy saw me walk in and instantly came up and said how sorry he was...Profusely!

I hugged him, and I said, "We ALL make mistakes...and I am sooo sorry that happened to you on your first day!"

I DO NOT share that, to pat myself on the back (far from it!) ...I share that to say,

"Hey!" ...I" need grace and mercy... and how can I EVER expect that from someone else, if I can't even give it out?!

"Even if it takes 2 weeks, 2 years, 2 decades...it is Never too late!

Life is not about
what 'THEY' do,
It's about what
'We Do', with it.

~Margie

❧ So...

I think God "stumped me" today.

(that's saying a lot)

Ashley.

Her name is Ashley.

Everyone has a name, even people who seem faceless.

This is a challenging one.

When you are "nudged", I fully believe it is for a reason.

A good reason.

Not sure where God is going with this...but I had the "nudge".

I was simply going to Kmart to return an item, when I drove by this girl (under a tree, way back in this huge parking lot, in the 90+ Florida sun).

Driving in my air-conditioned car, I passed her and went up to find a parking spot.

I had one thing on my mind.

Get in, get out, get home.

But when I got out and started walking to the front door, I got nudged.

It literally stopped me, but then I kept walking...

Really?

What's up with that?

I have a mission. A plan. But it stopped me again. So, I turned around.

Now I am walking in the blistering, scorching Florida sun, to the far back of the parking lot. I'm not sure why yet, but I'm certain there is a reason.

Her name is Ashley.

She is a stunning, gorgeous, tall, lanky, blonde "model" type... but somehow... I just sense she needs help.

So, I walk up and say "hi"...and I ask her "How can I help you? What do you need? "

She is a bit stunned, but I add, "don't worry, I'm not here to talk about God".

What made me say that, I don't know...it just kind of fell out of my mouth.

"I'm not here to talk about God"...

But she visibly becomes more relaxed, and says, "They all want to tell me about God. ALL of them. You name it!! But the Jehovah's Witnesses are the WORST!", and she sighs a huge sigh.

So, I ask her, "What do you need, how can I help you? "

But I'm already sensing Ashley is, let's say, very complicated.

So, I start by asking her if she'd eaten (I clearly see she hasn't).

She hesitates...

So, I say, "RIGHT NOW, if you could have anything to eat in the world... what would it be?"

She is quiet.

I see tears welling in her eyes, but also see she is clearly trying to be strong. So, I say, "don't think about it, what was the FIRST thing that came to your mind when I asked you? "She answered, with GREAT hesitance, "a steak".

I already could sense that she didn't feel worthy of a steak, so I said (with great enthusiasm) ... "And how would you like that cooked?"

Wow, the things we can learn if we just open our eyes...and follow a nudge.

Was this how "I" planned my day? No, not at all.

But now, I was on a mission to find her the best steak...

I don't go to the Golden Coral Buffet...no, no, no... I'm looking for the very BEST steak I can find!

And then, I stumble upon Outback! Perfect! (I think), and I walk out with a big juicy cut of filet, $24.00 later.

When I get back to the parking lot, she is gone.

I can't believe it.

She is gone. Even after I told her it might take me about 30 minutes to hunt down a steak, and I PROMISED I would be back.

Then, I realize...

She's probably heard many promises that have never come through.

So now, I go in search of Ashley.

When I find her, she is slumped over on a park bench staring at the ground.

I don't just drop the food and run along on my merry, planned afternoon... I ask her if she minds if I sit with her.

She sits straight up and smiles for the first time, and I suddenly see these piercingly, beautiful, crystal blue eyes…like the Caribbean. But then I see the depth of pain in them, and know I am probably in over my head.

She doesn't even touch the steak.

It could have easily been from the Golden Coral Buffet. And then, it hits me…it was never about a steak.

2 hours later I am, in fact, in over my head. (or so "I" think).

But I am determined not to walk away, because I know everyone else in her life has, and, because sometimes, people don't want to be "fixed", they just want someone to show them compassion.

It's like seeing someone sitting in a big huge mud puddle, and standing on the outer rim of it, telling them all the possible ways you can think of to get them out of it and get them "cleaned up". When in fact, all they really need is for someone to be willing to just come and sit down IN that nasty mud puddle, WITH them and LISTEN.

And so, as I sit there next to her, for another few hours, I watch her whole countenance change right before my eyes.

We are laughing together, and it is quite the transformation. She is COM-PLETELY excited, happy and smiling while telling me all about her 18-month-old baby boy, Jacob. She shows me the pictures of him that she carries in her purse, and with happy tears dancing in her eyes, she tells me that his first words were, "wub u".

She is clearly a loving Mother. It is clearly what keeps her alive.

And then, I suddenly notice…there are things crawling on her scalp. Glistening things.

She has lice.

LOTS of lice.

In this gorgeous, wavy, mane of glistening blonde hair.

Lots. Of. Lice.

Amazing how I sat right there next to her, for hours, and never even noticed this.

As her story unfolded, I just wanted to grab her and hug her.

Because that's "me". I am a huge hugger.

But I don't.

And that bothers me.

It really bothers me.

Honestly.

Because I know what it feels like to be sitting there, feeling unworthy of even the simplest act of a hug. To have to beg for compassion and see in someone's eyes that they are never going to come through for you.

Mother Teresa said it best: "We think sometimes that poverty is only being hungry, naked, and homeless. The poverty of being unwanted, unloved, and uncared for is the greatest poverty."

I am now desperate to find a hair salon to take her to, but I already know they won't take her.

I sense she knows that too, and my heart is broken for her.

Then she turns to me, tilts her head to the side, and almost childlike, says "I won't mind if You tell me about God. I think I would like that".

I am floored.

And for once, I don't know what to say, because I have been sitting so long in this mud with her, and, I suddenly fear I will mess it up and say the wrong thing.

I know, because I have been on the other side of that coin, and there have been people with the best of intentions who made me feel even worse.

I don't want that to happen to her.

Now, I am the one hesitating.

And for me, this is rare.

I don't start quoting scriptures to her, nor do I whip out a Bible, or break into a 12-step plan of Salvation.

I just start sharing my own story with her…and now she is wide eyed and completely floored that this woman, who looks like she has it all together, shares some very deep common threads with her.

And now I know why I was nudged.

It hits close to home, and this will be an awakening for both of us.

Finally, she starts eating the steak ravenously, as she listens.

Mother Teresa said,

"We are all pencils in the hand of God".

I would like to be bold and add…

NOT the eraser end.

~Margie

❧ So…

I have been getting to know a lot of my new neighbors over these last 8 weeks, and one woman's name kept coming up. Cindy. Each neighbor I met would say something like, "Oh, you'll want to steer clear of Cindy because she talks too much, and you'll never get away".

Hmmmmm. I instantly thought, I want to meet her. (Wow! I talk too much, too!)

But then someone else said "She's lonely", "her husband left her here and she keeps saying he's off camping", and the list grew.

One night, a neighbor invited me over for dinner on the deck, and while we were sitting there eating, my neighbor says "Oh just look at that!! She's out on her porch in her moo-moo again!".

I quickly sat up, and looked across the street and said, "Who is that? " Cindy? "We should invite her over to join us!!!!"

My neighbor looked horrified and said, "Oh no, she will talk like crazy!"

And I kind of chuckled and said, "Well, I talk a lot too, and I know what it's like to be lonely, and I know what it's like to be judged by those who don't know your story".

I got up, crossed the street, and introduced myself to Cindy.

I learned that she and her husband live in Maine, and this is a second home they come to.

She had been taking care of her Mother for the past 3 years until she just died before they came down in April. She said her Mother was her life-long best friend, and that she was having a difficult time handling the loss. She said she just couldn't go back to Maine yet, because she wasn't ready to face it. So, she asked her husband to go on without her until she was emotionally ready.

She's been here alone for 2 months now.

I went back to my neighbor's deck and shared the story.

That she had tears in her eyes.

That she said, "My Mother was my best and closest friend and she died last year, it is so hard to be without her."

"I never knew she was going through that all alone", my neighbors said.

Two days later, we all went out for dinner.

At the end of the night, my neighbor said, "Cindy, I didn't know you could be so much fun!"

She is now going to go visit her in Maine, when she feels ready to go "home" again.

"Do unto others as you would have them to do unto you".

We can go to a Church building every Sunday if we want, but what we do at home and in our day to day lives, is what really matters.

Let's try to help each other through our stories.

If you can be

anything you want,

Be Kind.

❧ So...

I got this wild idea this morning and started going door to door to invite neighbors over for "Monday Night Meatballs".

Tonight.

I decided I would stop knocking on doors, when I had 6 neighbors who said yes.

It was interesting. One woman said, "just don't ask that new lady who just moved in…she's an alcoholic!!"

Naturally, I got excited and said, "oh yay!" …and I proceeded to walk over to the new lady's house and invite her.

She was a bit stunned. She said, "well….no…. I don't think I can do that".

So I just chatted with her for a bit, and then I said, "Dinner is at 5:30 if you change your mind. I'd love to have you at least pop in and meet some neighbors".

Then, she looked at me and said, "Ok, I can pop in, but I won't stay and eat."

I said, "Oh good! THIS…is going to be SO MUCH FUN!!"

Here is how "Monday Night Meatballs" went down.

Too Much Fun! LOTs of Laughing! (we ALL need to laugh more! Seriously!)

Dinner @ 5:30…they all left at 10pm.

The woman who didn't want the new "alcoholic" neighbor to be invited… found out that they actually had a LOT in common!! (They are going to start walking on the beach together in the mornings!) Really.

I love it when we can "get it"!

Her husband of 40 years is dying of pancreatic cancer.

I said, "Oh my word! Is he at home??!"

She said, "Yes, but I told him that I am SO lonely and lost in all of this that I have GOT to find some friends!"

I jumped up, made him a plate of food, and started walking over with it.

I have NO idea how…but this frail man walked out of the house when he saw me coming with a plate of food and said, "I wanted to meet you half way. I saw you coming". (even now, I have tears in my eyes, writing that) Can you even imagine?

EVERYONE has a Story. I've known this since I was a little girl. I have a story. There were a LOT of "stories" last night!!!

And…here's what I came away with.

I think, instead of being in a checkout line @ the grocery store, or Walmart, or even the check in for a 5-star Resort… Whatever.

Unless you have lived a day in that "annoying" person's shoes… Being irritated, ticked off, disgusted….is, well….

Something, that we ALL could use a… "get out of jail free" card for.

❧ So...

I was in the grocery store tonight when I heard this small child's voice yelling.

I don't know what isle he was in, but he was yelling.

Yelling with excitement, is what it sounded like to me.

"MOM!!!! Look at THIS!!!, can we get it??!!"

He was loud and all over the place, but she stayed calm and patient. I remember those days with my own son and couldn't help thinking how cute it was.

As I got in line to check out, lo and behold, the boy and his Mom got in line behind me.

He was SO excited about everything he was seeing in the checkout line. Then, he started singing, happily...Disney songs. I was ALL in!

His Mom had a body like a stick figure, and she was pregnant. Way pregnant. The baby probably weighed more than she did. She was covered in tattoos.

People kept staring, with sharp looks of disapproval.

I just thought, "Oh Wow!!! I want to know the story behind all of those tattoos!"

They were pieces of art!

But I could also sense her awareness of people "judging" her.

She kept a smile on her face for her precious boy despite what people gasped about.

Yes, people gasped.

As if they even have a glimpse of who she is.

I didn't like it.

I loved that she was a calm and patient Mother who ignored the distaste of those around her.

I was proud of her.

And then, I had the "nudge" as I was paying for my groceries and I saw her pull out the WIC card.

I know the WIC card, all too well.

And I know the judgements that come from pulling it out.

You just want to crawl into a hole and die.

But you do it because you KNOW that you don't have any other options for the circumstances you are in. And there is no way in the world, as a Mother, that you will ever let your child down.

I swiped my card, and it asked me if I wanted cash back. I NEVER get cash back (there's no cash to get back, lol). But today, I pressed the buttons.

Holy Cow!!! I only wanted $20!!…It came up as $20,000 (thousand) bucks!! lol (slightly embarrassing moment, when it declined…but hey…)

Now, I'm getting the "look", from everyone in line that is irritated that I am so stupid. (except for the pregnant girl, who was actually, very consoling)

When all was said and done, and she paid with her "WIC" card…I turned around and gave her the

$20 bucks, and said, "This, is just a random act of kindness…and today… you're it!" She was floored.

She said, "No! you don't need to do that!" (and tried to give it back) (nervously looking back at the people in line, who were clearly DISGUSTED with this) I said, "I know, but, now it's yours…you deserve it", and I walked away. I share this because, unless you've walked a mile in someone else's shoes…

"WE DO HAVE THE POWER
TO RE-WRITE A LINE
IN SOMEONE ELSE'S STORY."

Jill Donovan, Rustic Cuff

So...

He looked like one of the scariest men I've ever seen, hands down...and he walked up behind me.

I almost didn't know if I could breathe for a moment.

Huge.

Solid.

Probably 6'4".

Full of tattoos... and scars that would make other men wince (and quickly look for an escape).

My brain quickly tried to set aside the sight of him and tried to adjust it, exponentially.

I took a deep breath, then quickly turned to say "Hi".

His face lit up (behind the massive, scruffy beard), and I was instantly, somehow, comforted.

How odd.

And then I noticed the horrific scars on his bald head. It's not like anyone could have missed them, they

are the kind that are blaring in your face and screaming an exorbitant amount of pain... that even Webster couldn't put a finger on.

So, I began chatting with him while we wait. (Me, and all my Pollyanna-like blinders)

What I got, was completely unexpected.

He'd been a sniper in the Army and got blown up overseas. Really blown up.

But here was the kicker.

He said, with what appeared to be watery eyes, (after I thanked him profusely for sacrificing for people he doesn't even know),

"Ma'am, I am proud to have done what I did for our country, I was one of the lucky ones.

I was just a boy from Alabama, with nothing and no one. But today I am blessed, and thankful to be alive.

I tell people who are brave enough to approach me, that I have no

anger, no resentment, for what has happened…. I just want people to understand that it's not about war".

And then he leaned way down and gave me the biggest bear hug I'd ever had.

ℛ So...

I check in on one of my elderly neighbors a few times a week. Not because I feel like I have to, or it's some kind of good deed that will get me some points with the big guy. I do it, because she is a little firecracker and I LOVE spending time with her (Insert BOATLOAD of stories here), and

I do it because she is all alone in that little trailer and I know what that's like.

We have become like two peas in a pod, even though there is a great expanse between our ages. After all, age is just a mindset.

And, for whatever reason, she ALWAYS sends me off with a potato.

Yes, "A" potato.

ONE, potato.

At first, I wasn't quite sure what to do, or say, when she ceremoniously plopped a potato in my hand on my way out her door the first time I stopped by.

It was…. well, let's just say, a new experience for me.

As awkward as it was, she INSISTED that I take the potato…so, I did.

I had NO clue why, but I did.

Her face lit up, and she was instantly. Happy!

Now, I was contemplating the meaning of potatoes.

I googled it. lol

What I learned, visit after visit, and potato after potato, was that it wasn't about the potato.

It wasn't about me.

It was about her.

HER need to GIVE. Her need to "Mother".

The JOY on her face, when she had the opportunity, it was her love language.

She is Irish.

Never turn away the gift of a free "potato" =)

❧2 So...

She was smoking the very butt of her cigarette, which she would stop periodically to try to relight. I don't know how she didn't set her lips on fire as she kept attempting it because there was nothing really visibly left of it. She was pacing back and forth outside of the Italian Restaurant, eyeing the front door and talking to herself. I couldn't hear what she was saying because I was sitting in my car waiting to go in and pick up my pizza.

She was carrying 2 backpacks, on her frail and filthy 80 lb. body. (I'm pretty sure the 2 backpacks weighed more than her).

She didn't look good.

At all.

Physically or mentally.

She must have paced 10 times before I got out of my car to go in. Obviously, something wasn't right with this picture.

So, as I'm standing at the counter paying for my pizza (mind you, this is an upscale Italian Family Restaurant, not Dominoes), I suddenly have this woman standing next to me with her bulging backpacks on.

All went quiet when she loudly asked for a handful of crackers (the look on the owner's face, and the rest of the workers…well, let's just say not the prettiest).

They are NOT going to give her a handful of crackers.

Me? I'm thinking, "Holy Cow!! This woman weighs all of 80 pounds and is hauling around 2 overstuffed backpacks, clearly walking the streets all day…she is going to need a LOT more than a handful of crackers to sustain her!!"

So, I turn to her excitedly and say, "Hey! I just bought a pizza! It's really hot, would you like some?", and I whip open the piping hot box, right there on their counter and grab her a plate.

I think the owner's eyeballs almost popped out of his head as his employee's stared at me in disbelief, and then back at him waiting for his wrath.

She looks a little hesitantly at the pizza (and them), and so I say, with enthusiasm! "Go ahead! Just take whatever you want!" pushing the box over a bit.

The sharp intake of breath by everyone in the restaurant was all that was audible at that moment.

Really. I mean WHO lets some filthy dirty crazy person just grab food straight out of their freshly cooked pizza box?

They all looked at me with disbelief as I just happily smiled and turned to sign my charge receipt (including a GOOD tip).

She was somebody's Daughter, somebody's Sister, somebody's Mother.

She didn't get there all by herself.

We didn't get where we are all by ourselves either.

We ALL need help.

Why did I leave a GOOD tip?

Because…Bad service + my Bad attitude… would have just equaled BAD.

I'm not going to buy into that equation.

Otherwise, there is no hope, for any of us.

It's not about
agreeing with people,
it's about accepting people.

~Margie

❧ So…

I was at a neighbor's house, having a cup of coffee, when I glanced out the window and asked, "Who is that?"

She looked out, and said, "ohhhh…. that's Nick. He's the new maintenance man for our co-op."

I said, "Oh yay!! We finally got a new maintenance man."

She turned around and said, "Ya…but when the snow birds return, they will NOT be happy!" I immediately asked why, and she said, "Well, he worked here before, and some people had a problem with the fact that he has SEVERAL tattoos…among other things…and then he got fired"

So naturally, I jumped up off her couch to run out and welcome him to our neighborhood.

He was a bit stunned, and obviously a bit taken aback, when I ran out and said hello.

But after I was chatting for a bit, he actually got a smile on his face.

That's when I saw he only had one tooth in front. A nasty, big front tooth.

I think there were only 3 others back in the molar section, but that was the extent of it. He was smoking little brown cigarettes like a chimney, and obviously very concerned about his appearance. Very Nervous.

But it didn't bother me, and I just kept chatting.

When I finally went back in to my neighbor's house I said, "What a kind man!" She just looked at me with a blank look on her face and said, "I just hope people will be happy with him being here when they return for the winter and find out he is back. They do not like his appearance in our neighborhood."

Fast forward 2 weeks.

This guy has been a non-stop WORK HORSE ever since he got here.

He will show up out of nowhere to tell an elderly person to go in the house, and he will clean up their yard work (even though it's not his job).

He will appear, out of nowhere, at 6am, to quickly clean up someone's garbage that the raccoons broke into and scattered all over during the night (again, not his job).

He goes nonstop all day long in excessive heat and humidity...wearing a LONG SLEEVE SHIRT and LONG SLEEVE PANTS.

Really??

So, I went to the Co-op Management and said, "This guy is doing an AWESOME job!! But I see he is sweating like a pig out there. Is there a maintenance uniform we can give him that is like shorts and a t-shirt??"

They looked at me kinda stunned and someone said, well...

Ok.

So, opened a HUGE can of worms.

But, I'm like...bring on the worms! (I've got a lot of Love, Grace, and Mercy to dish out...!)

It was his choice to wear the long sleeves and long pants, because he is afraid that he will offend people if he doesn't.

I'm sorry, but I am looking out the window of my comfortable air-conditioned home thinking... "somebody" has got to change this and make it right!!

Ok.

So..I'm going to be THAT "somebody"…and I will open this big can of worms!

Because, sometimes, people who feel like they don't have a voice (or feel like they don't have the LUXURY of having a voice) …don't.

I'm ready to get in the ring for Nick.

And I do!

IT IS UP TO YOU AND I.

~Margie

✿ So...

Today I saw an old lady struggle with a walker to go sit by the water.

She was impeccably dressed in white linen slacks and a beautiful sleeveless white silk blouse. The hat she wore was one of grandeur.

But she was alone, and no one came to join her.

I felt compelled to go say hello and sit with her.

She said had been visiting here for 5 weeks now, and that I was the first person who sat down and talked to her. It was her last day before she flew back home.

She had been coming to this place for 19 years with her husband but he, and all of their friends who used to join them, had passed on.

My heart broke for her as she shared story after story.

Two hours later I hugged her goodbye. We both had tears in our eyes.

No one should get to the end of their life and be sitting all alone.

I pray that I am not....and that someone would come sit with me too.

❧So...

First of all…let me just tell you that I am NOT a golfer.

Not because I don't want to be (because some of the most BEAUTIFUL places on earth are golf courses!) …but because I'm sure no one would have enough patience to deal with me shouting "squirrel"… instead of "fore"! lol.

Having said that, I find myself at a charity golf event on my day off.

I'm all about Charity!

They assign me to the 'Mulligan table' to sell tickets.

I'm good at selling…. I just want to know who Mulligan is so I can sell the most tickets for Charity.

Yep.

There you have it.

(at least I'm honest, lol)

Apparently, 'Mulligan' would be my Best Friend. =)

** a shot not counted against the score, permitted in unofficial play to a player whose previous shot was poor.

I'm thinking, WOW…that's awesome! How many can I buy?! (I might ACTUALLY be able to play golf with this guy Mulligan!!)

Then I think…Wow…how many 'poor' shots have we made in life that would have turned out differently if someone had given us a Mulligan?

❧ So...

I was at my art show opening when a woman came over, introduced herself to me and started chatting it up.

She'd just bought a house on the Island and is fixing it up. She needs some high-end art for it, she's looking at mine, and she loves it.

She tells me where she bought her place (beaucoup bucks) and continues to chat with me for quite some time. We seemed to hit it off.

Then, she pipes up and says, "Hey! Why don't we get together for dinner next week?!"

I said, "That would be great, I'd LOVE that!

She said, "Great! And, then, laughing loudly, adds "Just don't tell me you live in that trailer park!!...Can you even believe people live in that crap?!"

I smiled.

Big.

Chuckled, and said,

"Well...that's EXACTLY where I live!"

She was speechless.

Seriously. Speechless. Very uncomfortable.

But then, I handed her my business card (trying to help her out of the awkwardness of the moment--we've ALL been there) and I said, "It was nice to meet you. We both moved here not knowing a single person on the Island and I think it would still be great to get together sometime. Call me, if you need help with ANYTHING."

Never judge a book by its cover. Take time to read the story. It just might surprise you.

We had dinner this week, and we have a lot more in common than you'd think.

So...

What to do when you work with someone annoying:

Here is just my perspective, right or wrong. It's the lens I *try* to see everything in life through.

ALL of us can be annoying at times. Honestly. It really depends on the circumstances, but we are ALL human. If we all had it together and we were perfect...we wouldn't need a Savior. That's by no means a religious statement. It's just Reality.

It's where we ALL live.

This is what I always said to my Son when he was growing up and people were NOT nice (I still try to apply it today).

We are ALL in a different place in life. Our story is not their story.

Where we have been, is not where they have been.

Those are two completely different worlds.

Where we are now is not where anyone else is.

Try to see that annoying person as a Human (just like you and I). Realize that you have NO IDEA what on earth they have been through, or what they might be going through at this very moment.

MANY times, if we care enough to learn more...it is UNFATHOMABLE.

The fact that they can even get out of bed in the morning, and show up for work is a HUGE feat, in and of itself.

One that I think should be applauded.

Honestly, what I would do?? I'd invite them to lunch.

Seriously.

The thought of having lunch with an annoying coworker might make you cringe. That's understandable. Who wants to spend their lunch hour with such an annoying person?

But for me, as a little girl, I remember the Bible story about Zacchaeus, a wee little man who was the MOST DESPISED tax collector of the day. The IRS tear your hair out kind! lol

He climbed up in a tree, just to get a glimpse of Jesus. And then, Jesus showed up at the base of that tree and asked him to come down from there and have dinner at his house (people thought he was crazy!).

If you were Zacchaeus, wouldn't that just about freak you out??!

I mean, when we are annoying, we know it! (and when we are...we don't think anyone will love us like that!)

I think, it's just all boils down to Grace and Mercy.

We. All. Need. It.

Try to walk a mile in
someone else's annoying shoe's.

I say,
Invite them in,
And let them take their shoes off.

Mine are a little dirty sometimes.

~Margie

✂2 So...

I'm trying to get grip on this situation, FIRST.

If there's one thing I've learned in life this far, it's DON'T assume you know what's going on. Nine out of ten times, we don't.

Breathe for a minute (or 2 or 3 or...), but don't jump the gun.

Seriously.

We are NOT in their shoes.

I'm in the grocery store looking for laundry detergent when I hear this VERY loud man with an accent hollering a few aisles over.

He has a deep (loud and bold) NY Bronx accent.

He is obviously, distraught.

"I... SEEE REGULARRRrr, Pearl, Sport, SUPAHHHH..."

When I turn down this aisle, there is a man who is literally yelling into his cell phone "I DON'T KNOW WHAT THAAAHHH HELL I'M LOOK-ING FAAAA!!!"

There are people in the aisle, DISGUSTED, giving the evil eye, and now others, coming to the aisle, just to see what all the shouting is about.

I cautiously approach him.

His eyebrows seem to meet in the middle of his forehead as I start to speak.

I whisper, so as not to awaken the giant, "I can help you, I see you have a list"

He is silent.

The meeting of the brows tells me he doesn't get it. As if there is a hidden camera somewhere, he quickly searches over his shoulders, left and then right.

I see exactly what is written on the paper in his hand while he shifts from side to side, and I quickly grab the box he needs.

I smile, and I whisper, "Just tell her you've got it and you love her. NOW!!!"

He looks at me, eyes wide open, like he is about ready to jump out of his skin! (I'm thinking, Holy Crap, what have I done now?!)

I quickly go down the aisle in search of laundry detergent, all the while secretly praying he doesn't have a gun and I'm not on the 11 o'clock news.

He is clearly BEYOND distraught.

I have NO clue what's coming.

Then, there is a sharp tap on my shoulder. (I jump)

He hollers, "Whyy'd yah do that?!!"

I turned to him (smiling), and I said (very carefully), "Because I know that's probably a very hard place to be, and I just wanted to help you out."

He's speechless.

Like, dumbfounded, as his face contorts all sorts of looks.

And then, it all fell, like a puddle.

He looked at me with a boatload of emotion in his tough eyes as he barely got out the words, whispering, "My wife just got thaaa news that she's got breast cancahhh".

Never, Ever, judge a book by its cover.

If you don't know the whole story, don't even go there.

❧So...

I run in to Walgreens to grab a tube of toothpaste real fast, when this little ole man comes shuffling into line in front of me.

He turns around, smiles at me, and says playfully "It's your lucky day, you got behind ME!"

I laughed and said, "Take your time".

He gets this huge smile, showing off his beautiful pristine dentures. (I'm sure he was quite the Lady's Man in his day when I see him flash this smile at me). The woman ringing him up asks him for his rewards card.

He looks at her, looks at me, then says "This might take a while!"

People are piling up behind us, hemming and hawing (it's Saturday for Pete's sake!! Everyone wants to hit the beach asap!!)

He turns to me and says, "See how lucky you are today?"

I laughed, light heartedly, and said "Oh, believe me...I am."

But I can almost feel the unspoken words of disapproval in a few people behind me, to which I turn to all of them (with a "party kind of attitude") and say "Hey! Someday we will ALL forget where we put our reward cards! So, I hope people can have some patience when it happens to me! I know I'm gonna need it!!!"

Then, after the little ole man is searching his suspender assisted pants, the cashier says "Ok, well, if you can just give me your phone number I can put that in for you".

He laughs.

Yes. He laughs, and says, "WHAT, is my number?!"

I think people are wanting to throw their own reward cards at the cashier at this point. But then, he suddenly spouts out a phone number which the Cashier punches in, and then she exclaims "You just earned a coupon for $3 towards anything in the store!!".

He looks at me, with a grin.

I look at him, smiling, as he tosses this $3 coupon proudly in his bag and this little ole lady comes up to him at the register (they are both shorter than me! lol) (ha! yes, hard to imagine). I quickly say to him, "Hey! You should give that $3 coupon to your wife before you lose it! I'll bet she can find something for 3 bucks in here!" (I'm quite amused when the entire line of people waiting to check out, nod in agreement.) Now…he's REALLY showing off his pearly whites, as he ceremoniously hands her the $3 coupon!

She is, of course, ecstatic.

She hands him $18 in change from what she purchased at the store next to Walgreens and disappears.

I say to him, as I'm checking out, "Whoa!!! You just got $18 bucks for a $3-dollar coupon!!" He chuckles, like a school kid, and says "Ya, took me over 50 years to train her to do that!!" And now everyone is laughing….

When, she comes around the corner with what she wants to purchase with her big $3 win. No joke…

Two BRIGHT , FLUORESCENT YELLOW beach noodles (they are 2 for $3).

I high five her.

They are 81 and on their way to the beach.

Priceless.

❧ So...

I was juried in to a two-day Art Show, and excited, because the quality and level of Artisans in this show (27th year) is really high. I am honored to be among them this year.

But, at the end of the first day it was a total wash for ALL of us.

It was unheard of. THOUSANDS of people were expected, and maybe 200 showed up on the first day. I'm now convinced this is where the term "starving artist" comes from.

But I'm trying to walk around, be positive, and tell the other Artists that the "thousands" will show up the next day.

Didn't happen.

So now I'm asking God, "What's up with that? What am I doing at this show?"

And then...this woman walked up to me, with her beautiful teenage daughter.   She is looking for something she says.

She just doesn't know what.

Her daughter picks up one of my beach photo cards and asks if she can get it.

She looks at her Daughter and says, "I'm not sure I want a memory from here."

Then her daughter points to a Canvas Giclée that is hanging and exclaims with excitement, "This is the one Mom!!" (it's a beautiful beach sunset)

I look at her and I say, "That one is called *Sunset at the Sandbar*".

And then her Mom's jaw drops, and tears start welling up in her wide eyes. "REALLY?!! Are You Kidding Me?!!"

I go over and put my hand on her shoulder and try to comfort her, although I don't yet know the cause of the overwhelming emotions she is clearly feeling.

She starts to wipe her eyes and apologizes profusely while her teenage daughter looks on, horrified that her Mother is crying to a stranger.

I say, "No...don't apologize...it's ok...just go ahead and cry."

Then she says, tears streaming, "My Wedding was just cancelled at the last minute. He's gone. The Sandbar was where he had proposed to me, and where our Wedding was supposed to happen Christmas Eve. I plucked my daughter out of her Senior year, to re-locate here for his new job. People had paid for plane tickets, and hotel rooms. My Parents booked Christmas week to spend time with us as a family in our new home..." (she is sobbing now, under her dark sunglasses).

So, I do all that I know to do.

I hug her.

And she starts bawling.

She is not a stranger. She is a Human Being, with Hopes and Dreams.

She is in a new place where she doesn't know anyone yet, and her whole world has just shattered.

Her teenage daughter looks at me, warily, probably kind of embarrassed her Mother is doing this with a total stranger.

But me?

I embrace it all.

I look at her daughter, and say, "I am SO Proud of you!!! You had to walk away from everything you knew and start over. That's huge!"

Then, I look at this crying woman, and I say, "I understand where you are at. I have been in places where I was SO embarrassed at the unexpected, UNBELIEVABLE, turn of events in my life, that I have just wanted to crawl under a table and die".

She stops crying for a minute, and looks straight in my eyes, and says, "Really?"

"I shouted at God today" she adds, as she is waving her hands wildly in the air. "What's up with this?!!!" I have NO business being here!

But my Daughter begged me to get us out of the house and stop hiding.

Then we stumbled upon this art show.

I didn't want to look at anything. I've just been walking around in a daze, until I saw your photos.

I look at them both and I say, excitedly, "Ok! THIS...is where it all turns around. Right here.

You might not want a memory from here...but here is what I think: THIS can be the turning point.... where you take what was meant for bad...and turn it into GOOD!"

"I would love to get together with you for coffee tomorrow!"

She looks at me now with these bright, wide, tear blurred eyes and stunned, asks, "Really?!"

I grab the beach photo card and I put it in a bag and hand it to her daughter as a gift.

Her embarrassed teenage daughter actually hugs me and says,

"Thank you for talking to my Mother!"

Me?

I remember very clearly times when I have sat in my car in random parking lots…sobbing.

All alone.

Devastated.

Embarrassed.

Praying to GOD someone would show up and just hug me.

It has nothing to do with money.

Money cannot buy Compassion.

Ever.

Compassion…Is FREE.

It's not the wrong size or color.

And, no one will ever stand in a long line to return it.

We had coffee for 3 hours the next day.

❧So…

I'm in the grocery store, and it is packed like a can of sardines.

The shelves look as though there is a hurricane coming. Forget butter, milk or bread. It's NOT happening today.

I get to the checkout (long lines out the whazoo) and people are quite irritated.

When it's my turn to put my stuff down the young boy (of 6ft tall!) says enthusiastically,

"So how is YOUR day going?"

I reply, "Fabulous!!".

He stops ringing.

He looks at me.

"Really?!"

I enthusiastically say, "YES! It's another beautiful day on the Island and I'm happy to be alive!".

He looks stunned, scans another item, stops again.

He asks, "You live here?"

"Oh Yah!!!" I say with gusto, "How fortunate is that?!!"

He looks at me very seriously now and says "You have NO idea how many people come through and complain all day long. They are tired of all the tourists. They are miserable. But I always try to lighten it up and point out all the good things."

Now I stop.

I look at him.

I see his name tag.

"DJ!" I say, with excitement..." YOU ARE AWESOME!! I Love your attitude!!!" I mean, this kid is 17! He could be hacked off that he has to deal with all these complaining people, but instead he chooses to try to lighten up their day.

I jump up and smack him a high five (I have to jump, I'm only 5ft tall lol), and I practically shout,

"Thank You for having such great attitude!! You made my day!"

He gets this big grin on his face and when he turns to the rest of the people waiting in line we both see that they are all smiling now, and their attitudes have changed. I love when that happens.

Attitude is highly contagious.

Make yours worth catching today.

❧ So...

She is 81 and hit a hole in one today.

She does Yoga on Tuesday's.

She does water aerobics on Wednesday's.

And, she'll tell you exactly what she thinks.

Point blank.

So, I asked her what word of advice she'd like to give everybody.

"Give it up".

"There's no time for crap".

And there you have it.

No charge.

Short and sweet.

❧ So...

He is angry.

And by angry, I mean L I V I D.

L I V I D.

I am quickly feeling like I was instantly shot out of my shoes, unaware, and not quite sure how to put them back on.

I am in the checkout line at Kmart, just trying to buy toilet paper on my way home.

He turns around and SCREAMS at me (waving his arms wildly), that I am "in his space"!!!

This is a new one for me, but I try really hard not to react and just start apologizing profusely for the "invasion" (because I know it's probably got nothing to do with me).

Based on the look on his face, he's a bit puzzled by my response, but I'm thinking, "Holy Cow! There HAS got to be more to this!"

So I am polite and kind (while honestly a tad bit concerned I will get shot in the parking lot on my way out) ....BUT....I try to lighten the move by striking up a lighthearted conversation with him while the cashier looks on, horrified.

(Hey, I might get shot in the parking lot...but at least I will have died being kind to someone)

He does a double take at me over his shoulder as he pays for his purchase.

I just smile back.

Then I walk out the door to find him standing there.... apparently waiting for me.

We have all been hurt,

broken, or lost,

at some point in our lives.

Let's try not to add to that.

~Margie

So...

My neighbor (whom I've never met), arrives from out of town at his rental property next to me, which apparently, he checks on once a year.

I go over and excitedly say, "Hey! I'm Margie, your new neighbor" (and I enthusiastically extend my hand to shake his).

He instantly yells at me (yes, yells) "Your palm tree is encroaching on my space!!!".

Ok then.

I retract my hand (because he refuses to shake it), and try to quickly assess this situation" BEFORE uttering a single word (that I cannot erase, take back, delete from a text, etc.)

It's a challenge. I just bought this place a year ago, I didn't plant the tree, and I am pretty much blown out of the water on this one.

So.

I try to muster up some grace and mercy and reply, "I'm so sorry. Let me check on that for you. I am new in the neighborhood. I'm really not sure who owns what, and where the property lines are yet, but I will check on that".

He screams at me now.

In my face.

"I want to add a screened in porch, and YOUR palm tree is blocking me from doing that!". Okaaaayyyy...

Again, I try to stop my head from spinning and think straight for a minute.

What's really going through my mind is, "HOLY CRAP!!! How much does it cost for a Palm Tree Relocation Program?!"

I don't know.

But what I DO know at this stage in life is that it's probably got nothing to do with the palm tree.

So I acquiesce.

I am more than happy to help fix his problem…as he sees it.

He is a tad bit confused. He obviously has no clue how to respond to my gesture.

I think his face, demeanor, and sudden loss of speech kind of summed up the fact that no one has probably ever not fought back.

I'm good with that.

Either way.

Doesn't matter to me.

He is my neighbor.

BUT THAT'S NOT FAIR, you say!

Nah.

Nothing in life is fair.

THAT, my Friends…Is Step 1.

And now?

The palm tree still stands, and he actually surprised me, and power washed my house for me while I was away at my Dad's funeral.

Love wins.

❧ So...

It's 10 pm and I hear a knock on the door.

I get out of bed and open it to see a neighbor standing there in her pajamas with a bag in her hands.

She seems distraught.

She hands me the bag and I take a peek.

It's a can of frozen lemonade and an onion.

She said this is what's left in her house.

Onions and a frozen can of lemonade.

She wants me to have it.

She doesn't have Alzheimer's. She just said she is sad and saw my light on. (Actually, it was just the nightlight in the kitchen...) She really needed someone to talk to.

I quickly invite her in... and then, I excitedly tell her I LOVE her pajama's! (because I do)

(*note to self, I need some new pajama's!)

So.

We are both in our pajama's and we are both exhausted. It's after midnight now.

But we both start laughing because I look pretty silly sitting in my jammies in the living room, holding a bag of onions and a frozen can of lemonade after midnight.

The only recipe for that combination is…well…something I think we all need to whip up.

I'm glad she knocked on my door.

"Loneliness
and the feeling of being unwanted
is the most terrible poverty"

Mother Teresa

❧ So...

I took my neighbor out for a Birthday lunch today.

We had a GREAT waitress.

Full of life, full of spunk, and completely present to cater to your every whim.

HAPPILY!

I chatted with her. I wanted to know how long she'd been doing this.

She said she started in Philly when she was just 20.

Her birthday was yesterday. She is now 48 and has 3 kids.

She's been "serving" her whole life.

She's smiling like CRAZY…with nasty half blackened and broken teeth.

Her happy attitude is contagious.

It is a STUNNING dockside restaurant on the water. Big boats pulling in.

Incredible ambiance, decor, and service.

She runs out to greet them and take their order.

Takes back drinks, and they start yelling at her.

She comes back in the door, SMILING, looks at me and says, "I've been through a LOT of HELL in my life…. but I make the CHOICE …every day to be happy! If a customer is nasty, I just try to rub that *happy* all over them!"

I high five her.

She's my kinda girl!

❧So...

I don't know why it happens, but it does.

It's kinda crazy that way.

When I am having a particularly challenging day, someone amazing crosses my path.

Like the stunning, drop-dead gorgeous, beautiful woman I saw today.

She was flawless.

And she had no legs.

Her smile was so radiant, that you didn't even realize she is missing both legs.

And then, my world is instantly shifted back into perspective as we share an elevator ride, chatting and laughing for a few floors.

When we get off, I have to high five her in her wheelchair, because she made my day.

Now, when I look down, my legs don't look so fat to me anymore.

❧ So...

When I got in the car with her, she informs me she is on suicide watch. 24/7. Not because she didn't want to live anymore, but because there just wasn't anywhere else to go at this juncture.

I listened to her just spill it all out, without any filters.

No more "Band-Aids".

Because there becomes a point that you are so covered in "Band-Aids"(and still bleeding to death), that there is not an ounce of energy left in your body to continue to just slap another one on.

It's not like someone just pulled up to a drive thru and placed an order for it.

Like, "Hey...I'll take an order of fries....and Oh! can I pick up a side of horrific abuse and debilitating depression to go with that?".

Super-size it.

That is her reality.

So, when she finally pulled into a parking lot and stopped the car, I turned to look at her and asked, "What do you need right now?"

She looked straight at me with instant disbelief that she could have any-thing, and quickly responded, "SERIOUSLY??!!!"

I said, "Yes! WHAT, at this very moment, do you need?"

She looked at me, one eyebrow slanted in disbelief, and practically shouted at me

"HONESTLY?!!"

I practically shouted back, "Yes! Honestly! Nothing is off the plate".

After a moment of silence, she responded with an exhausted wariness and hunched shoulders, in almost in a whisper...

"All I ever wanted in life was a family"

My heart clenches. My eyes water.

And I instantly get it.

So, I ask her, "...and what does 'Family' mean to you?"

She replied, "Hanging out, playing games, cards...baking pies...I've NEVER baked a pie."

5 hours later, we are sitting on my kitchen floor, laughing.

I had never baked a pie either.

It's very simple.
Be good to people.

It's not rocket science.

~Margie

❦ So...

I met a Mother in the hospital who was there with her Son who was 5 and dying of cancer. He had already had a bone marrow transplant and she was sitting by the side of his hospital bed, now 8 months pregnant.

She gave birth there a few weeks later and was breastfeeding her new baby boy in a chair next to her 5-year-old Son's hospital bed when he passed away before her.

I asked her what she needed.

She looked at me with tears streaming down her face and replied with an answer I wasn't expecting.

A baby dresser.

In this darkest hour at the hospital, a baby dresser didn't make sense. But I have learned that a lot of things in life don't make sense, because the "reality" you are living is so "unreal".

I don't try to say, "Well, how about I go get you some food to eat instead, I think you need food etc..."

I come back with a card (money in it) and tell her to go buy a dresser.

She looks up at me, tears still streaming down her face, and says, "Really? Thank You!! I kept promising my Son that someday I would be able to buy him a dresser, so his clothes weren't always just stacked on the floor. Now I can give that to his little Brother."

She could have told me she needed a kitten and I would not have questioned it.

It's not up to me to decide what she needs.

"Anyone

can find the dirt in someone,

Be the one that finds the gold."

Proverbs 11:27

❧ So...

I just babysat a two-year-old foster child whose Mother had just been arrested.

Allegedly the child's father is one of the biggest drug kingpins on a most wanted list (I don't know drugs, and I am not even sure I got the lingo right on that...but...).

The Foster Parents told me that they had someone trying to beat their door down in the middle of the night. So, they called the Police.

"Don't answer the door for anyone!!" they say.

I'm thinking, "Oh Crap!"

They leave.

Immediately I try to lighten it up for him, and I turn on "Little Einstein's" to watch before I feed him.

I'd never seen/heard of that program before, but the Foster Mom said he is REALLY intrigued by it....so I put it on.

He is mesmerized.

There are a bunch of different chickens running all around like crazy, and then this one animated character says very animatedly to the other...

"Don't you judge your chickens, till you've been inside their coop".

❧2 So...

One of my new neighbors was hosting a little hors d'oeuvres party last night.

I walked in and suddenly realized I was probably the only one there that was under the age of 80.

I spent 4 hours talking to husbands with broken backs, wives with severely sagging skin, couples who have all been married for over 50 years, beat cancer (sometimes twice), faced the death of a child, lived through the depression with "not even 2 nickels to rub together", yet all still together.

At one point I was sitting next to one fun couple on the couch who were wearing color coordinated outfits and laughing a lot, when all of a sudden, he pipes up with his booming voice and says, "Of ALL of the decisions I have EVER made in my life...", he hesitated, and the room fell silent... "Marrying HER was the BEST THING I EVER DID!!!...that was 59 years ago." And he just beamed.

And then he quickly added, "Oh! And don't think it's perfect!!" He chuckled heartily..."NOTHING is Perfect!!! We just had a big blow out over something yesterday!!" lol

"BUT here's the thing", he says, as he is pointing his finger around the room at everybody, to drive his point home....

You love them MORE than THAT.

❧2 So...

I'll be a bit vulnerable here.

About 2 hours ago, I finally broke down and started crying.

Not my finest hour...but just an overly exhausted one.

I was not able to work for the past month because I came down with a severe case of bronchitis, that turned into walking pneumonia...and then I broke a rib (from coughing so hard in the middle of the night... and then it just went downhill from there.

I live alone.

No medical insurance (Obamacare turned me down last year, and I am not old enough for Medicare)

I've spent the last week flat in bed, in excruciating pain, with a heating pad on my ribs (I have read 5 books, and completely missed Christmas)

So today, I just started crying.

I just said "God...all I need right now is a rotisserie chicken from the grocery store...

is that too much to ask?" (I was sooo hungry!)

Laugh if you may, but that's just "me".

I'm real. I'm honest. I just tell God how it is.

A rotisserie chicken is my "go to comfort food". (well, bacon…bacon is too…but I'd been sick for so long I needed protein, I hadn't eaten in days)

2 hours after that, I get a knock on my door.

It's my atheist neighbor.

Painfully, I get up and answer it, thinking she needs me.

But lo and behold, she says she was out to see the new Star Wars movie and then thought on her way home that I probably couldn't cook with a broken rib (so she stopped to grab something).

She handed me a bag and left.

I just opened the bag.

It is a rotisserie chicken.

❧ So...

If there's one thing I know and have learned in life, it's that when you are doing the right thing FOR SOMEONE ELSE it all works out. Like even when it shouldn't, and the odds are against you. Because it would be like finding a needle in a haystack.

There is this kind of inner voice that shows up out of nowhere and says, "I gotcha covered"....and then BAM!!.... there you are in the middle of that haystack holding that needle!

This Mother was one of those needles.

I was in the midst of mind-blowing poverty, in Sri Lanka, looking to meet the people of the village.

Soon they were coming out to the dirt road before I even got to them (probably to see who this crazy white lady was lol) and then there she was... smiling, with that precious baby in her arms. I think she was smiling because she knew. She KNEW...just like I did.

There is no greater feeling than when someone shows up for you, because words are not necessary. It's a universal language.

She took me into her dwelling, gripping my hand as if not to lose me again, and picked up a shabby black and white photo to show me. She had the hugest smile I had ever seen when she pointed at it and said something in Sinhalese.

The interpreter looked at me and translated "THIS man is why I smile".

Her eyes even smiled.

And then I learned that it was her husband and he had just died.

If there's ever been a moment when everything that seems blurry comes into such a sharp, clear focus, this was it.

Until my eyes filled with tears for her.

But she was still smiling so big, and never skipped a beat (or let go of my hand), as she told the translator to tell me, "It's ok, it's ok, it's ok".

And then I got it.

I witnessed and experienced it.

Life isn't about our circumstances, it's just about our hearts.

It's a choice.

In the end, it's not about what we have. It's about who we are.

In this moment, she was one of the richest women I had ever met.

Standing on a dirt floor in her windowless dwelling, without running water, and a hole outside to relieve herself in…smiling like she was a Queen living in a palace.

"We can't help everyone,
But everyone can help someone."

Ronald Reagan

❧ So...

She yelled out to me in the dark desperately holding her head, "I have MASSIVE head pain!!!" This between horrific coughing attacks, and broken speech that practically render her senseless.

She whispers, "I'm sorry".

"No! Don't be sorry!! I am here!", I whisper back.

It is dark, it is 3:00 a.m. and we had been up since 1:00 a.m.

I gently take her hand and smile at her.

"It doesn't matter what time it is," I reply. "I'm here. Don't worry".

I go to her kitchen and get her a dose of Tramadol and a big glass of water (she is on the maximum dose, until Hospice comes).

It's not touching her pain.

It's overwhelming.

It is Easter morning.

People will be rushing to get to Church on time, checking that their shoes are the 'perfect match' for their Easter outfits and making sure the kids look perfect.

Nothing is perfect.

If it was, we wouldn't need a Savior.

❧ So...

As I am approaching the bus stop bench with my grocery bags, I quickly see him come into clearer view. He's over 6 feet tall, weighs about 280, and looks to be about 48 years old.

I instantly sense that something is a little "off"…but I go ahead and set my bags down on the bench and sit down. Immediately, and very loudly, he rips the earbuds out of his ears and points wildly at my bags.

"I DON'T BELIEVE IT!", he blurts out, "You have fried pickles in your bag!!!"

I smile (excitedly) in response, "Yes!! Yes, I do! I LOVE fried pickles!!"

He then mimics my big smile with a childlike goofy kind of innocence and blurts out, "I've never had them!!" and then reaches up to yank his ratted ball cap over to the side of his head like a boy of five.

"This is the second time today I have seen someone with fried pickles! What's up with that? ", he asks with wide childlike eyes.

I chuckle, smile, and say, "They are on sale!"

Then, this huge presence of a man quickly turns his nose up like a child and says, "That doesn't sound very tasty to me."

So I begin to share my "culinary expertise" on the awesomeness of fried pickles. I very excitedly gave an impromptu verbal dissertation on fried pickles, off the cuff, and quite animatedly I might add.

He is now following my every word, soaking it up like a sponge, smiling like crazy, when he whips out a mini recorder and starts to dictate (no joke)…

CLICK: "Apparently, fried pickles are the BOMB!!"

He quickly glances at me for verification. I nod with a smile, and so he continues…

"I have it on a very AUTHORITATIVE word, and recommendation that I MUS T try these!" CLICK.

CLICK: "Oh, and my 'source' says to be sure to dip them in ranch dressing!" CLICK.

And I high five him (we all need high fives in life…validation/acceptance of the diverse places where we are).

And then, as the trolley approaches I quickly pull out the box of fried pickles and give them to him to take home and try.

He practically jumps out of his skin with excitement, clapping like a big kid.

"REALLY?!!" He shouts, ecstatically. "You are just going to GIVE these to me? !"

Yes, Yes, I am! (I'm jumping up and down now with this giant of a boy in his excitement.) He is over the top.

Then he hops on the bus like the happiest kid on earth, clapping and shouting to all the passengers, "I JUST GOT FRIED PICKLES!!! I JUST GOT FRIED PICKLES! WOOHOO!"

All I am thinking is,

"Oh, Dear God, if we could all just be that happy about simple things, like fried pickles."

❧ So...

I was driving to the store to pick up a Gingerbread House Kit to mail to my son and his wife for Christmas. It is a tradition that I started with Kristopher when he was only two-years-old. We would decorate one every year while singing (loudly) to our favorite Christmas songs. He would then ceremoniously write our house # over the door of the gingerbread house in frosting, and I would take a picture photo of him, smiling wildly and holding up the gingerbread house. There are about 16 of these photos (with MANY different house numbers).

For me, as a Mother, no matter what had happened that year, no matter if we had to leave a home in the middle of the night (for safety) and leave everything behind, I was determined to make the tradition of the ginger-bread house happen for him. Because, you can't put a price tag on time spent together.

Today, I am driving, and I am contemplating what I will do on Christmas Day.

I am alone in the trailer.

It's the first year in my life that there are no decorations, no tree, no Christmas cards to send out, no gifts to send...except for this gingerbread house kit. Because THIS is what truly matters to me.

As I am driving out of this huge shopping center parking lot full of frantic shoppers, I pass by the big Lowe's Christmas Tree tent and I spot a wom-an, about 29 years old, holding a sign.

I am kind of in a hurry to get home, but I get this huge nudge that tells me I should go back and talk to her and see what she needs.

As I'm turning around to go back I'm thinking to myself, "I wonder what she needs…maybe I should go get a gift card over at Panera first".

But when I park and get out and I actually get a good look at the cardboard sign she is holding, I get EXCITED! Yes!

I run over and ecstatically say, "Oh my word!!! Your sign says you NEED a Tree!!!!"

She looks at me, and shyly replies, "Yes ma'am".

I start clapping my hands excitedly and exclaim, "YAY!!!!! Let's go find you a tree!!!!"

She gets this big smile on her face, and replies, "REALLY?!"

I say, "Um YAAAAA!!! This is going to be FUNNN!!!"

(At this juncture, she probably thinks I'm crazy, but I don't care).

We walk into the tent, and I look at her and say, "Pick whatever tree you want!" Mind you, I really don't have money in my budget for this tree, but I know I need to go out on a limb here (pun TOTALLY intended!)

She stands still. The expression on her face tells me that she almost doesn't know what to do with that kind of luxury. She hesitates at first, but when I start to ask her if she has kids (to ease her wariness) she INSTANTLY lights up!

Now we are effortlessly chatting about our kids, and being a Mother, and just life, when I suddenly exclaim, "Oh my word! You will need a tree stand!! Let me run back into the store and grab one and I'll be right back to pay for the tree!" When I return, she is the only one in this huge tent, standing silently with the Lowe's man.

They both look uncomfortable. Very uncomfortable.

But me? I am THRILLED! So, I excitedly ask her what tree she picked.

The Lowe's man shifts from side to side and looks down at the ground.

She, very quietly says, "Well, I didn't know what price to look for, so I'm not sure."

So, I look at the Lowe's man and excitedly ask him, "What tree was her FAVORITE tree?"

They both glance at each other, and then he sheepishly points, and hesitantly says, "Well...THAT one."

I got excited, clapped and said, "YAY! We'll take it!!!"

She starts crying.

She looked at me with tears still in her eyes and said, "Everyone who has stopped... said I didn't "NEED" a tree.

They would say, "Let me give you FOOD...THAT's what you NEED. You don't NEED a tree!", or "You need Jesus!". All the while, they are here buying a tree to take home...

"I actually NEVER dreamed that anyone would ever really buy me a TREE! I can't believe you did that for me! THANK YOU!!!!!"

We ALL carry signs through life.

Maybe not on a street corner, but we ALL carry them.

We need to learn to READ each other's signs.

THAT....is where the GIFT truly lies.

It has nothing to do with money.

She needed a tree.

I needed a gingerbread house kit.

❧ So...

Her hair was half shocking purple, half fuchsia, with bright lime green streaks in it.

Double nose rings.

Double eyebrow rings.

I had passed by her many other times before, always sitting alone, always on that same bench. NEVER holding a sign.

She was always just sitting alone.

Today, I passed by her again and I just knew I had to turn around, pull over, and go sit with her.

So, I did.

It seems we were both alone on Christmas Day.

She was the sweetest girl I have ever talked to.

She did not want anything.

She said she understood she didn't deserve it.

I said, "Oh, I'm not here to give you anything. I'm all alone on Christmas Day too, and I have seen you sitting here before and so I just thought I would stop and say 'Hi', and Merry Christmas."

So, we just sat and chatted about life for a bit, until this guy came flying by us on his Harley with a Santa hat on. When she turned to watch him go by, I saw the tattoo on the back of her neck.

It said "Bella" in fancy script with hearts and flowers.

Some people would say, "What the heck is wrong with that girl for putting such a gaudy thing on the back of her neck?!! That's disgusting!!"

I said, "Oh! Who is Bella"?"

She looked at me, with a blank look--an *I don't know you lady, not sure I can trust you with that info* kind of look.

I quickly said, "Oh, that's ok...you don't have to share that if you don't want to, I understand..."

Silence.

Then she looked at me and said, "Ok...you want to know who Bella is? She is my little girl who is an angel now."

I said, "What a beautiful tribute to her, that you carry her with you!"

She looked at me, kind of questionably, and then turned to stare off in the other direction. (giving me full view of "Bella" again), then sharply turned back to face me.

She said, "The reason I put her there on the back of my neck was that... THAT is the place where you can instantly die if it snaps, and it is severed. SHE is holding it together for me!! I snapped I thought I would die when she did, but I am still here because of her. I have to LIVE, for both of us."

She sits there, every day, because if she went home she would be beaten, and left for dead. Sitting alone, on a bench every day is a luxury for her. I understand that luxury.

People will say, she should just get out of there!

They might think she is stupid for staying.

I say, unless you are living in her shoes, and unless YOU are the one willing to take the risk to get her out of there, it's easy to speculate.

People can dress up in suits and ties all day long…

But unless we choose to speak life, it really doesn't matter what we are wearing.

❧ So...

I'm going to preface this story with the fact that my Dad always instilled in us growing up that, no matter how much money you have or what your status, it is VERY IMPORTANT to leave things better than you found them.

To this day that mandate rings very clear to me, and I've never been able to walk away from ANYTHING without hearing his words resound in my ears.

1. Don't walk into a restaurant bathroom (I don't care if it's 5 stars) and complain about a messy counter when you are washing your hands. (You are fortunate to HAVE hands!) Simply wipe it up when you are done (and don't be too proud to do so). Smile when you walk out.

2. Don't go into a dressing room and try on a gazillion things without putting them back on the hangers properly. (Yes, people get paid to do this, but you are no better than them, and you are not having to pick up after people all day long for minimum wage either)

Today, I helped my 71-year-old neighbor who has owned a cleaning company all her life (and is not well). We cleaned three massive gulf front homes. (Rents @ $6,000 a month)

Thank God my Dad taught me well!!

Upon arriving at the 3rd home (after working like sweating pigs all day on the first 2), we found the couple checking out late. Wayyyy late. They should NOT have still been there and my neighbor was quite irritated.

Trying to diffuse the tension, I start to chat with them about where they are going home to, etc. The wife apologizes profusely (over and over) for being SO late getting out.

I see the pain in her expression when she apologizes.

And I feel her pain when I see her husband of 47 years in the wheel chair she is pushing.

✂So...

He found a quarter!!!!

He was just 5 years old, so this was a huge find and a HUGE deal...because you could get a GIANT gum ball from the big gum ball machine... with just a quarter!

You know... the one where you put the coin in and then it shoots down the spiraling tube and all the blinking lights go off and on and you just know you have won something good.

He kept that quarter in his pocket all day, treasuring it like it was a piece of gold.

And then we stopped at a traffic light and saw a very pregnant woman holding a sign.

I glanced at him in the back seat and said, "I think we should go through that McDonald's drive thru and take her some food".

He shook his head.

"No, Mommy! We need to go home and make her KRAFT macaroni and cheese!".

I'm thinking...Okkaaaayyyyy...KRAFT?? (this was a LUXURY item in our home)

We did not have money for Kraft at this time in life.... but he INSISTED she should have KRAFT.

Apparently, he knew the difference between the bargain brand and Kraft…at age 5.

So, we went home and made Kraft macaroni and cheese.

I'm pulling out some plastic silverware when he loudly insists, "REAL SILVERWARE"!!!

We only had 6 place settings. Five was going to be just one less than the perfect set.

We took the REAL silverware.

We took it in REAL Tupperware.

We took hot KRAFT macaroni and cheese.

She was gone.

Ok…End of story.

NOPE. Not on this five-year-old's watch.

We finally found her on another corner (looking like she was ready to give birth at any minute).

We got out and started chatting with her as she wolfed down the hot Kraft macaroni and cheese…when all of a sudden, he reached deep into his little boy pocket and pulled out the quarter.

I had no idea what he was doing….

And then he handed her his treasured quarter and said, "This is for the baby when it comes out".

This, my friends, was the day I TRULY learned to GIVE WITHOUT LIMITS.

"Unless you become like little children…"

May we all learn to live with one less place setting.

I think
the moment we realize
it's not all about
'me'
…is the moment
that Real Life truly begins.

~Margie

❧ So...

She loves Harley's and Jack Daniels (on the rocks).

She is 71.

She shows up every afternoon to work impeccably dressed (with full makeup and hair done).

She works 3-10 PM…SIX NIGHTS A WEEK!

She is definitely tougher than nails in a coffin.

I love her already.

But they all call her the "Old Bitch".

They steer clear of her.

Well, first of all, I'm going to say right off the bat that she is not just an "old bitch". She is weathered and worn…and rightly so.

Her Son fought in Vietnam. He came home pretty much unrecognizable she said.

So she nursed him and took care of him for years…and then he committed suicide.

She said she has lived every single day of her life since that moment dying inside and angry at herself… because she failed as a Mother to save him.

"Walk a mile in someone else's shoes" doesn't even begin to scrape the surface here.

Because it's not just someone else's shoes…. it's someone else's hell.

"Shoes" cannot even begin to describe what she has walked through in over 70 years.

I'm going to have to take mine off.

I think we all should.

❧ So...

They are in their 80's, and they've been married 61 years.

(That's longer than I've been alive, lol)

Being me, I always have to ask…"What's the secret?!" (I always want to know!)

She pipes up, with MUCH enthusiasm, and says, "Oh! It's NO secret!!! Let me tell ya! THIS lil' stinker gets out of bed at 5:30 EVERY morning! (and I catch a glimpse of the "caught-red-handed look" on his face)

She adds…"Go ahead…ask me WHY!".

I give.

"Why?"

She nearly SHOUTS the answer at me.

"Because I told him when we got married, that the last one out of bed has to MAKE it!!!!

Do you think he has ever had to make it?? Nooooo! Because, when I get up, IIIIIIII…I make it!!….and THEN… he goes back in and lays on TOP of it… ALL MADE UP!!!!"

And she slaps her knee hard, to make the point!

He looks a tad bit GUILTY (but with a little mischievous smirk on his face).

And so I ask her, "So what on earth do you do when he does that??!!!"

She looks at me, very calmly now, and says, "Nothing!

"NOTHING?!", I ask in shock.

She quickly replies, "He's lucky he's still alive!!!, His Mother thought he'd be dead by 40! I'm just thankful to see him still breathing!"

Real.

Life.

People.

THIS, is where it is at.

Perspective.

Then...He spoke up from out of his guilty silence and said, pointing at her, "SHE...is the BEST Thing, that ever happened to me! My Mother was right, that I should have been dead by 40...but I have "HER", and he points... with a huge smile on his face and a twinkle in his eye...as he looks at her.

And this, my friends, is 61 years, of mercy and grace kind of love.

❧ So...

He was wearing only one shoe. The leg without a shoe was swollen, reddish purple, marbled, and about three times the size of the other one (which was about the size of a stick).

This is what I encountered early in the dark this morning as I approached the business to unlock the door.

I quickly had to reassess my first thought...that no one was around.

It was still dark, and he looked as though he could harm me, but I continued to the door without fear.

I knew he had a story.

He actually picked these flowers for me before I went in and asked me if I believed in Jesus.

I haven't had a man give me flowers in six years.

And just last night, I had walked by the flower section in the grocery store and said, "God, I would really love to have someone give me flowers again! I miss that, God".

I walked into my office and stuck them in my water cup, turned back around to go out the door and thank him again. Only a few minutes had passed, but he was nowhere in sight.

He had simply disappeared.

Every day, we make choices.

Every day we have the choice to curse under our breath,
the person who cut in line.

Every day we have the choice to curse drivers on the road
who are not 'as competent as we are'.

Every day we pass by homeless people,
who we are sure are 'working the system'.

Every day we have the CHOICE to speak life or death…
about people's whose stories…
we know nothing about.

What's your story?

~Margie

Made in the USA
Columbia, SC
21 October 2018